OVER 450 YEARS AGO

IN THE NEW WORLD

PHILIP SAUVAIN

ILLUSTRATIONS BY

ERIC ROWE

new
Discovery
B·O·O·K·S
New York

Maxwell Macmillan Canada
Toronto

Maxwell Macmillan International
New York • Oxford • Singapore • Sydney

First American publication 1993 by New Discovery Books, Macmillan Publishing
Company, 866 Third Avenue, New York, NY 10022
Maxwell Macmillan Canada Inc., 1200 Eglinton Avenue East, Suite 200, Don Mills,
Ontario M3C 3N1

Macmillan Publishing Company is part of the Maxwell Communication Group of
Companies

First published in Great Britain by Zöe Books Limited, 15 Worthy Lane, Winchester,
Hampshire SO23 7AB

A ZOË BOOK

Devised and produced by
Zöe Books Limited
15 Worthy Lane
Winchester
Hampshire SO23 7AB
England

Printed in Italy by Grafedit SpA
Design: Julian Holland Publishing Ltd
Picture research: Victoria Sturgess
Illustrations: Eric Rowe
Production: Grahame Griffiths

10 9 8 7 6 5 4 3 2 1

Library of Congress Cataloging-in-Publication Data
Sauvain, Philip Arthur.
    Over 450 years ago : in the New World/Philip Sauvain; illustrations by Eric Rowe.
        p. cm.—(History detective)
    Includes bibliographical references and index.
    Summary: Describes what life was like in America before the coming of the Europeans
and examines the effect of the arrival of Columbus, Pizarro, and Cortez on the lives of
the native peoples.
    ISBN 0-02-726327-4
    1. America—Discovery and exploration—Spanish—Juvenile literature. 2. Indians—
First contact with Europeans—Juvenile literature. 3. Incas—History—Juvenile literature.
4. Aztecs—History—Juvenile literature. [1. America—Discovery and exploration—
Spanish. 2. Indians—First contact with Europeans. 3. Incas—History. 4. Aztecs—
History.] I. Title. II. Title: Over four hundred fifty years ago in the New World. III. Title:
In the New World. IV. Series.
E123.S2   1993
970.01'6—dc20   93.2649

Photographic acknowledgments

The publishers wish to acknowledge, with thanks, the following photographic sources:
7, 11 Ancient Art and Architecture Collection; 12 Werner Forman Archive/National
Museum of Anthropology, Mexico City; 14 Ancient Art and Architecture Collection;
18t Peter Newark's Western Americana; 18b The Hulton-Deutsch Collection; 22 The
J. Allan Cash Photolibrary; 26t Ancient Art and Architecture Collection; 26b The Hulton-
Deutsch Collection

Cover inset Werner Forman Archive/Museum für Volkerkunde, Vienna

CONTENTS

"*Tierra! Tierra!*"—"Land! Land!" At dawn on October 12, 1492, the crews on three Spanish ships went wild with excitement. Land had been spied ahead. After weeks at sea, they had reached Asia—or so they thought!

In fact, they had found America. They were the first Europeans to do so since the Vikings 500 years earlier. The leader of their expedition, Christopher Columbus, had been sure they would reach Asia if they sailed west from Spain. Finding a new way to trade with countries like India, Japan, and China was very important to people in Europe at that time. They got silk and spices from the East. But by 1492 wars in the Middle East had slowed down this trade.

Columbus knew that the world was round, but he thought it was smaller than it really is. He did not know that America and the Atlantic Ocean, as well as the Pacific Ocean, stood between him and Asia. He thought Japan was only 2,500 miles (4,000 kilometers) from Spain instead of 12,000 miles (19,200 kilometers). It took Columbus, an Italian, seven years to get money from the rulers of Spain to pay for the voyage.

Columbus and his crew set sail from Spain in three small ships—the *Niña, Pinta,* and *Santa Maria.* After leaving the Canary Islands, they sailed westward across the Atlantic. For more than a month the sailors were out of sight of land. Some were afraid they would never see Spain again. Columbus told them lies to hide the fact that they were so far from their homes.

"People from heaven"

Days before Columbus saw America for the first time, he and his crew saw clues that told them land could not be far away. They saw a floating branch with red berries. Birds flew over their ships. They even saw a carved stick. Columbus landed first on an island in the Bahamas, close to the coast of what is now the United States. He called it San Salvador ("Blessed Savior"). The arrival of the Spaniards came as a shock to the Native Americans who lived there. Since they thought they were the only people on earth, this meant the Spaniards must be gods. "Come! Come to see the people from heaven!" they shouted.

Columbus made many mistakes. He was so sure he had reached India that he called the Native Americans "Indians." When he sailed to Cuba he mistook it for China. He thought Hispaniola was Japan. It was here that the *Santa Maria* struck a coral reef just below the surface. Columbus made the best he could of the accident. He used planks from the ship to build a fort called La Villa de Navidad. He named it after the Nativity, because the shipwreck took place on Christmas Day. Columbus left 39 men in charge. Then he returned home. His news of a New World caused a sensation in Spain.

When Columbus landed on the island he called San Salvador, the local people came out to greet him. They treated the Spaniards like friends.

The Native Americans who
lived on the island belonged
to the Arawak people.
Their chief was called
Guacanagari. He came to
the rescue of the Spaniards
when the Santa Maria was
shipwrecked. He sent people
in canoes to help the
Europeans save the planks
from the ship.

Fifteenth-century Spanish coins like this have been found
in the Caribbean. They could have been taken there by
Columbus in 1492 or by sailors some years later.

Where did Columbus land in the Bahamas, a
group of over 600 islands? Some people think
"San Salvador" was, in fact, Watling Island.
Others think it was the island of Samana
Cay. Both islands fit the description that
Columbus wrote down: "The island is large
and very flat with green trees and many
waters and a large lake in the middle." There
is no proof that Columbus landed on either.
What do you think would really prove
that Columbus landed on one of these
islands? Does finding an old Spanish coin
prove that Columbus
landed there?

HISTORY DETECTIVE

The 39 Spaniards at La Villa de Navidad were the first Europeans to settle in the New World. When Columbus came back to Hispaniola eight months later, however, he discovered that his fort had been burned down by the islanders. The Spaniards he had left in charge were greedy people who became angry with one another. They had murdered many of the islanders and stolen their goods. In revenge, the islanders had killed all the Spaniards. Yet, when Columbus first went to the Caribbean, he had said, "I cannot get over the fact of how gentle these people are." The Arawak people carried few weapons apart from the spears and arrows they used for hunting and fishing. The massacre at Navidad had put an end to any lasting

friendship between Europeans and Native Americans.

When he first arrived in the Caribbean, Columbus said about the islanders, "I know they are a people who can be made free and converted to our Holy Faith more by love than by force." "They have so little to give," he wrote, "but will give it all for whatever we give them."

The Native Americans who lived on the Caribbean islands were farmers. They lived in palm-thatched houses amid fertile fields. They grew corn, beans, and sweet potatoes. Those who lived near a river or by the sea also made a living from fishing. They made speedy canoes by scooping out tree trunks. They had no industries apart from the weaving of cotton cloth and the making of pottery.

Newcomers bring misery

When Columbus visited Cuba, some members of his crew went to a large village of about 50 houses. They saw something there they had never seen before. Men were smoking rolled up tobacco leaves. "In order to take their smoke, having lit one end, by the other they suck and receive smoke inside with their breath," he wrote.

Columbus looked closely at the way the Native Americans lived together. He said, "It appears to me that the women work more than the men." They lived in groups, each with its own chief or king. Columbus made friends with some of these chiefs, such as Guacanagari.

The Native Americans smoking cigars on Cuba were the first people we know about who smoked the leaves of the tobacco plant. The words "tobacco," "barbecue," and "maize" have all come to us from Native American languages.

Soon many other Spaniards came to the Caribbean. They treated the Native Americans as if they were animals. They used their guns to hunt down men and women and force them to work on their plantations and in their mines. A visitor named Bartolomé de Las Casas

Some of the descendants of the people Columbus met still live in palm-thatched villages today.

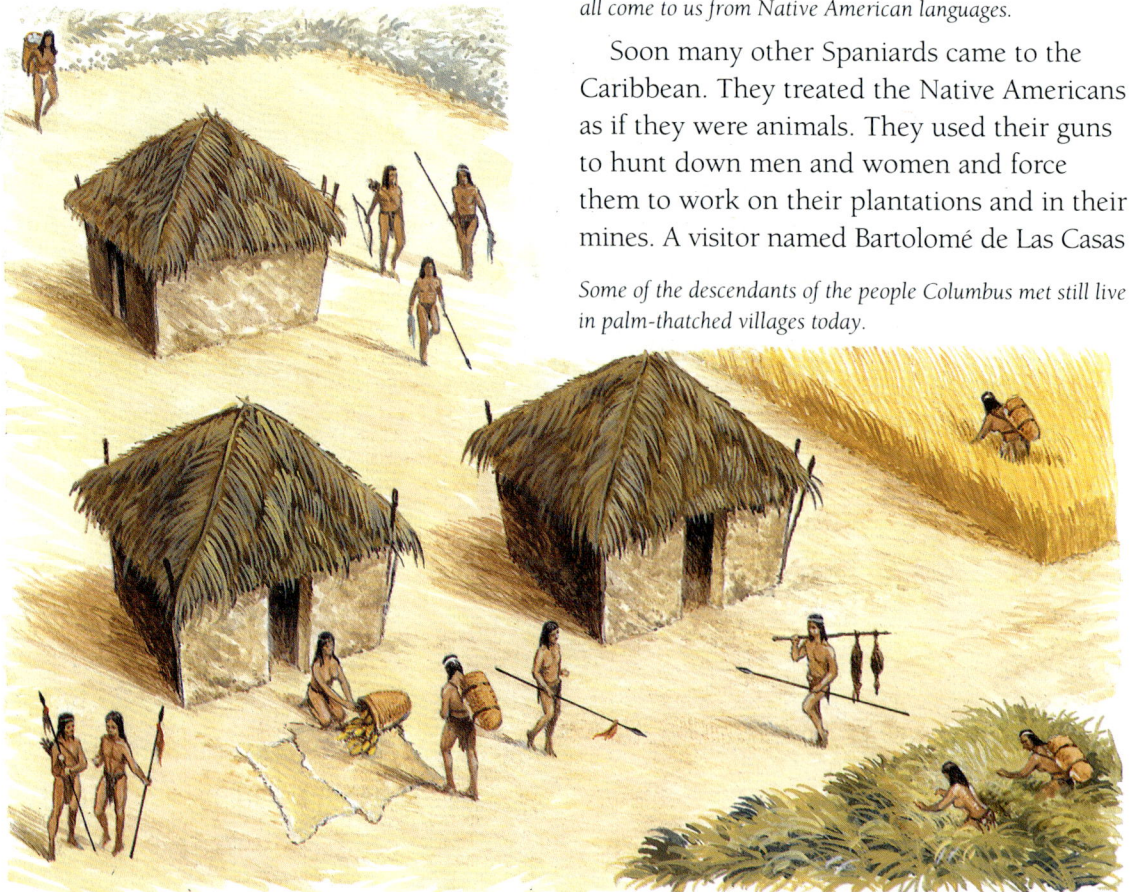

This is a map of America published in 1540. It shows what was then known about the American continent. Europeans called both North and South America by a Latin name, Mundus Novus or Novus Orbis. This means "New World." Soon mapmakers were able to draw exact maps as explorers traveled around the coasts and made more and more journeys inland.

We know a lot about the lives of people in the past from the remains found in burial grounds. Experts can say how people died and tell how old they were at the time. Skeletons found in Cuba and Hispaniola show that many Native Americans died soon after 1492 from diseases that had not been known before in the New World. Even simple illnesses, such as measles, can kill people who have never faced these germs before. Some experts think that as many as a third of the 300,000 people living in Hispaniola in 1492 died or were killed within four years of the arrival of Columbus and the Spaniards.

was horrified. He wrote, "The Spaniards with their horses, their spears and lances, began to commit murder and strange cruelties. They entered into towns and villages, sparing neither the children nor old men."

Soon most of the Native American workers had died or been killed. The European settlers replaced them with black slaves who had been taken from their homes in Africa. The Africans were sold to slave traders and shipped across the Atlantic to work on the sugar cane plantations of Cuba and other islands in the Caribbean.

THE AZTECS OF MEXICO

The European discovery of the New World destroyed many Native American civilizations. In Mexico the Aztecs were ruled by the Emperor Montezuma. He was the high priest of their religion as well as their king. Montezuma lived in Tenochtitlàn, one of the greatest cities in the world at that time. It had been built on an artificial island in the middle of a lake. Bridges and three earth causeways connected it with the shore. The streets and canals that criss-crossed the city were lined by buildings painted in bright, dazzling colors. Peasants used the canals to bring food to the great market in the city. Barges carried vegetables, maize, beans, pumpkins, chili peppers, tobacco, cocoa, and cotton. Many of the homes had shaded courtyards with fountains to keep them cool. Montezuma's fine palace was filled with every luxury. It even had a private zoo, a beautiful garden, a large fish pond, and a massive aviary where he kept hundreds of tropical birds. The most important building was a large pyramid in the city center. This was the main Aztec temple and the hub of their religion. It was surrounded by a wall.

This is the great "calendar" stone from the great pyramid in Tenochtitlàn. The Aztec priests used it to forecast eclipses of the sun. In the center of the stone you can see a mask depicting the sun god Tonatiuh.

13

Religion

The great temple of the Aztecs was in the center of Tenochtitlàn. This gigantic pyramid had a great flight of steps that led up to the twin temples on the top. The Aztecs believed that the spilling of human blood was needed to make sure that the sun rose every day. The priests used flint knives to cut out the hearts

The great pyramid was the religious center of the Aztec people. Over 80,000 humans were sacrificed there in 1487.

of the human victims who were sacrificed on the great stone of the temple.

Religion was very important in the lives of the Aztecs. They worshiped the war god

This Aztec ornament, a two-headed serpent, is studded with jewels. Today it is displayed in London's British Museum.

The main market in Tenochtitlàn was the place to which Aztec merchants came from all parts of Mexico. Slaves were on sale here, along with turkeys, fruits, and other goods.

Huitzilopochtli, who was said to speak to the people through the priests. Each year the Aztecs held military ceremonies, such as the flowery wars when thousands of soldiers wore gaily colored war dress, masks, and helmets covered in feathers. They fought mock battles with one another. They carried round shields made from reeds and were armed with spears tipped with flints, wooden-handled swords with sharp stone blades, and bows and arrows. Games and entertainment were also part of their religion. They danced to music from flutes and drums and played a violent ball game called *tlachtli*. The players wore special clothing to protect themselves against injury.

Today, Mexico City is one of the world's largest cities. It has been built on top of the site of the ancient Aztec capital of Tenochtitlàn. Archaeologists digging at the site of the great temple, in the city center, found a huge round slab of stone. This had been carved to look like a god. The dig also uncovered the walls of a temple and the remains of human sacrifices. Many other Aztec treasures have been lost. Priceless gold ornaments were melted down by the Spanish so that they could be shipped back to Spain more easily. Some Aztec treasures, such as this serpent ornament, were kept in one piece. What does a find like this tell us about the life of the Aztecs?

HISTORY DETECTIVE

CORTÉS AND THE CONQUISTADORES

 News of the great riches to be found in the land of the Aztecs reached the Spaniards who had settled in Cuba. A soldier named Hernán Cortés prepared to lead an expedition to Mexico. He landed at a place he called Vera Cruz on Good Friday, April 1519.

Cortés took with him a small army of just over 500 conquistadores, together with 16 horses and seven guns. Bernal Díaz del Castillo, who went with Cortés, explained why they had come. We came "to serve God and His Majesty," he said. "And also to get rich," he added. News that strangers had landed was taken to the emperor Montezuma. He had been warned by priests that one day strangers would bring his empire to an end, so he sent ambassadors to greet them.

The Aztec messengers gave Cortés valuable presents such as huge round slabs made of solid gold and silver. They were a bribe to make Cortés go away. Instead, they only made him keener than ever to find their gold. When the Aztec messengers returned to Tenochtitlàn, they described the white stranger with his beard. The Aztecs thought that Cortés must be a long lost god called Quetzalcoatl. Their legends said he had a beard and white face and would come back in the year they called *Ce Acatl*—1519.

This old map of Tenochtitlàn was drawn soon after the Spanish conquest of the Aztecs. It shows the shape of the Aztec capital and its unusual position in the middle of a lake. One of the Spanish soldiers called it "the most beautiful city in the world." It was also probably the largest and the cleanest. Road sweepers swept its streets each day at a time when most European streets were muddy and filthy. The Aztecs used an aqueduct to carry water from distant springs to the city.

MEXICO, REGIA ET CELEBRIS HISPANIÆ NOVAE CIVITAS.

Siege

Hernán Cortés was the most famous of the Spanish conquistadores. He went to Cuba when he was only 19 years old.

Meanwhile, Cortés had decided he would take his men deeper into the land of the Aztecs. His tiny army was armed with guns. He was sure they would be strong enough to defeat the Aztec armies with their primitive weapons. But, in order to show his men there could be no turning back, he burned all but one of his boats. The remaining ship was used to send gold back to Spain and to get royal approval for the expedition.

In order to reach Tenochtitlàn, Cortés had to pass through the lands of a Native American people called the Tlaxcalans. After fighting against Cortés, they joined forces with him to fight their enemies the Aztecs.

The Tlaxcalans and the Spaniards marched

18

Aztec soldiers dressed in all their finery. They fought fiercely against the conquistadores, but they had no guns.

together toward Tenochtitlàn. Before they could attack the city, Montezuma sent messengers inviting Cortés to enter Tenochtitlàn. Once inside the Aztec capital, however, Cortés took Montezuma prisoner and seized control of the city. When the Aztec people and their warriors gathered in huge numbers for a religious ceremony, the Spaniards panicked and killed thousands of Aztecs. Montezuma tried to stop the fighting but was killed by his own people.

Cortés lost a third of his men as they fought their way out of the city. Soon he returned with reinforcements. The Spaniards laid siege to the city and stopped food and fresh water from reaching the people of Tenochtitlàn. After three months the Aztecs had to give in. The Spaniards pulled down the buildings and temples of the city and did their best to turn the Aztecs into Christians. They destroyed the Aztec way of life for good.

After destroying Tenochtitlàn, the Spanish built Mexico City in its place. Many Aztec documents were also destroyed. A Spanish bishop burned a great pile of Aztec books. He said they were writings of heathens, people who do not worship the Christian god. This is why there are only a few written records that can tell us about the Aztecs. These picture books have drawings that show what their clothes and customs were like.

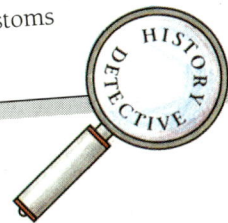

HISTORY DETECTIVE

The Spanish also destroyed the great Inca empire in South America. It stretched for 2,500 miles (4,000 kilometers) along the Andes Mountains from what is now Ecuador in the north through Bolivia and Chile to Argentina in the south.

The Inca empire was long, narrow, and very mountainous. At its center was the area we know today as Peru. This empire had been built up in less than 100 years. Between 1438 and 1527 the Inca emperors of Peru had conquered many other peoples. They ruled this empire with the aid of a well-trained army of soldiers. Their warriors fought in battle to the sounds of blaring trumpets and war songs. They fought with spears, bronze-headed clubs, and slings. They wore helmets and carried round shields to protect their bodies.

The emperor lived for part of the year in a thatched palace in the center of the great Inca city of Cuzco. This was built 11,500 feet (about 3,500 meters) above sea level. Only the emperor and the leading nobles and officials were allowed to live there. Ordinary people had to live in twelve villages on the outskirts of the city.

The Incas built fine roads through the Andes. Runners carried the mail along these highways. They could bring news to the emperor quickly from all parts of the empire. When the emperor traveled, he sat on cushions on a litter, a box with a roof of feathers carried on poles.

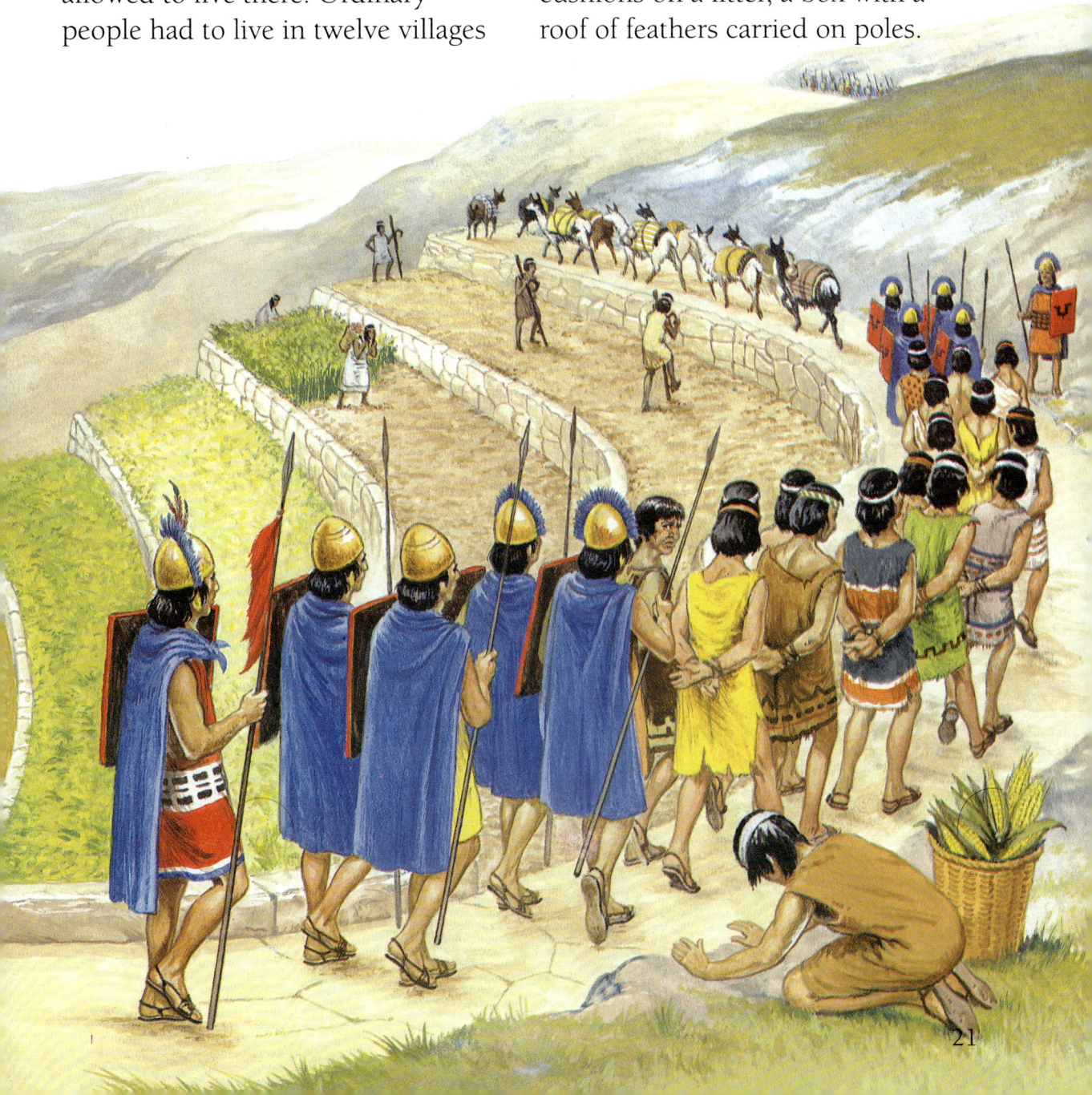

Most of the Inca people lived by farming. The mountain slopes were steep. The farmers often cut terraces into the hillsides to make flat areas of fertile soil on which to grow their crops. These included corn, beans, potatoes, and peppers. They kept flocks of llamas and alpacas. These are animals like sheep with a thick woolly coat. The Incas used the wool to make cloth.

Cuzco

Each year the peoples who had been conquered had to send gifts as tribute to the Inca emperor in Cuzco. The gifts they made were of precious metals, such as gold and silver, or goods made by crafts workers. They included richly decorated cloaks and embroidered cloth. The emperor's clerks kept records of the amounts that people paid on knotted strings called *quipús*. The emperor used some of his great wealth to build paved roads, temples, forts, and bridges throughout his empire. Irrigation ditches were also built to enable farmers to bring water to their crops.

The people who worked in Cuzco included

This paved Inca highway is near Lake Titicaca, high in the Andes. Despite the fact that the Incas had no horses and no vehicles with wheels, they had a superb road system. At this time the roads in Europe were muddy and almost impossible to travel on. The Inca roads, by contrast, had firm foundations and were paved with stones to make them long-lasting and easy to walk along. But only the emperor and his officials could use them.

The greatest highlight of the Inca year was the annual Festival of the Sun, which was held when the sun was directly overhead. This was the start of the Inca New Year, a time of joy and celebration.

civil servants, clerks, tax collectors, porters, fishermen, crafts workers, weavers, farmers, musicians, architects, and soldiers.

Four great roads met in the center of their city. There was a fine central square where the people could gather in front of the Temple of the Sun to worship the sun god. The temple was covered with gold plate to make it shine like the sun.

The Inca religion was not as bloodthirsty as that of the Aztecs. Incas worshiped the sun, moon, and stars and sacrificed animals, such as a white llama. Only rarely did they sacrifice human beings as well. They used a carved stone to tell them when the sun was directly overhead. This was the period of the Great Sun Festival. Only the highest ranks of society, the nobles, were allowed into the Golden Enclosure of the Temple of the Sun to worship the god. The rest of the people stood outside.

Some remains of the Inca civilization can be seen today. You can still walk along parts of the roads that once threaded their way through the steep valleys of the Andes. Why do you think the Incas went out of their way to pave these roads with stones? Hanging rope bridges crossed the deep river gorges. Some of these Inca bridges are still in use today, although the ropes have been replaced many times. They were made by stretching six long ropes across the valley. Four of these ropes were covered with matting to walk on. The other two held up the sides of the bridge. As you crossed over, it sagged in the middle!

HISTORY DETECTIVE

The Inca civilization was destroyed by Francisco Pizarro about ten years after the defeat of the Aztecs in Mexico. Pizarro was a Spanish soldier like Cortés. He first went to America in 1509. When he visited Panama, he heard tales of a fabulous empire called Tahuantinsuyu to the south. It was said to be filled with gold and great treasures.

Pizarro set out to conquer Peru in 1531. His four half brothers went with him. Pizarro was greedy for gold. This surprised the Incas. One of the Inca warriors once asked Pizarro if the Spaniards ate all the gold they were given, since they never seemed satisfied! Pizarro and the Spaniards had another aim. They wanted to turn the

Incas into Christians and make Peru part of the Spanish empire.

Pizarro led an army of 177 soldiers armed with guns. About a third of them rode on horseback. They landed in the north at a time when the Inca empire was split in two. Huáscar, the rightful emperor, and his half brother Atahualpa had been fighting a bitter civil war. Atahualpa had only just taken Huáscar prisoner when he heard news of Pizarro's advance. Messengers told him that soldiers had arrived in a "big ship from out of the sea, with animals, like llamas, only larger." Pizarro crossed the Sechura Desert and climbed up through the snow-capped mountain peaks of the Andes. With his tiny army he marched on the town of Cajamarca where Atahualpa had set up camp.

Treachery and death

Atahualpa was interested to know what the Spaniards looked like. He was not afraid of them and arranged to meet Pizarro. Atahualpa went unarmed, in a solid gold litter, into the main square of Cajamarca on Saturday evening, November 16, 1532. At first he could not see the Spaniards and thought they must be afraid. But the Spanish soldiers were hiding in the houses surrounding the square. When Atahualpa arrived, they jumped out and massacred 6,000 of his followers.

The Spaniards took Atahualpa prisoner. Later, in desperation after months of imprisonment, he agreed to pay a huge ransom in gold to secure his release. His followers went to every part of the empire to collect enough gold and treasure to fill a room 22 feet (6.7 meters) long, 17 feet (5.2 meters)

This is the cover of Felipe Guamán Poma de Ayala's chronicle of Inca history, which he wrote about 400 years ago. It is one of the few written records that tell us about the life of the Incas.

wide, and 9 feet (2.8 meters) high.

To his shame, Pizarro did not keep his part of the bargain. He was afraid to let Atahualpa go. His tiny army of Spaniards was greatly outnumbered by the Inca armies. He had seen how ruthless Atahualpa could be. He had even ordered the execution of his own brother. Would the Inca soldiers allow Pizarro to leave peacefully with the gold once he let their emperor go? So, even though Atahualpa had kept his word and paid the Spaniards a huge fortune, Pizarro put Atahualpa to death.

After executing Atahualpa, Pizarro seized Cuzco. He let his soldiers plunder the treasures of the city. The Inca people were unable to stop them. Nor could they stop the Spaniards from taking over their lands. They were forced to work as slaves on the Spanish

This picture shows the powerful Inca emperor Atahualpa. We don't know exactly when he was born. It must have been about 1500 in what is now Quito, the capital of Ecuador.

The murder of Atahualpa by the Spaniards was an act of treachery. Many more were to follow. For hundreds of years after the landing of Columbus, Native Americans were enslaved and killed.

farms and plantations and in their mines. The Spaniards treated these Native Americans with great cruelty. Those who put up any resistance were executed. Many were burned at the stake. The Spaniards also made the Inca people give up their worship of the sun god and turn to Christianity instead. They built abbeys and churches in Peru and pulled down the old Inca temples. In doing so, they destroyed the way of life of the Inca people. It was the end of one of the greatest civilizations to be founded in America before the coming of the Europeans.

The cruelty of Cortés and Pizarro and their supporters in destroying these civilizations was copied by many of the other European invaders and settlers who took away the lands of the Native Americans in the centuries to come. Even today, the way of life of the native peoples of the Amazon rain forests is under threat.

The history of the conquests of the Incas was handed down to each new generation by word of mouth. Fathers told their children about it. People called "rememberers" were paid to learn it by heart. How are stories of the past handed down to succeeding generations today? Luckily, an Inca who was related to one of the nobles put down on paper some of the stories he heard. Felipe Guamán Poma de Ayala wrote his picture chronicle of the Incas about 400 years ago. He illustrated it with many pictures of Inca warriors, battle scenes, women at work, crafts workers, and emperors.

HISTORY DETECTIVE

1438	Pachacuti becomes Inca emperor and together with his son Topa Inca begins the conquests that made the Inca empire one of the largest in the world at that time
1451	Birth of Christopher Columbus in Genoa, Italy
1478	Birth of Francisco Pizarro at Trujillo, Spain
1485	Birth of Hernán Cortés at Medellín, Spain
1485	Columbus seeks the support of King Ferdinand and Queen Isabella of Spain
1492	Columbus sets sail from Palos on August 3
1492	A lookout on the *Pinta* sees America for the first time on October 12. *Santa Maria* wrecked off the coast of Hispaniola. Columbus builds La Villa de Navidad.
1493	Columbus returns to Spain in March. In September he begins his second voyage to the Caribbean.
1493	The Pope divides rule of the New World between Spain and Portugal
1498	Columbus lands on the mainland of South America on his third voyage to the New World
1500	Portuguese explorer Pedro Alvares Cabral discovers Brazil by accident
1500	Birth of the Inca emperor Atahualpa in Quito, Ecuador
1501	Amerigo Vespucci sails along the coast of South America. His name later is used in the word "America."

1502	Columbus makes his fourth and last voyage to America
1506	Death of Christopher Columbus at Valladolid, Spain
1509	Pizarro arrives in America
1511	Cortés is among the Spanish soldiers who conquer Cuba
1519	Cortés lands at Vera Cruz on Good Friday (April). Defeats the Tlaxcalans in October. Enters Tenochtitlàn in November.
1520	Montezuma is killed in June. Cortés and the Spaniards have to fight their way out of Tenochtitlàn. The Portuguese explorer Ferdinand Magellan sails into the Pacific.
1521	Tenochtitlàn falls to Cortés
1527	Pizarro's first landing at Tumbes in northern Peru. Death of the Inca emperor Huayna Capac. His son Huáscar becomes Inca emperor in his place, but another son, Atahualpa, begins a rebellion.
1531	Pizarro's second landing at Tumbes. He sets out to conquer Peru.
1532	Atahualpa defeats his half brother Huáscar
1532	Atahualpa taken prisoner by Pizarro on November 16
1541	Pizarro murdered at his home in Lima, Peru
1547	Death of Cortés near Seville, Spain

ambassador: a person who represents a ruler or a government at meetings with other governments

aqueduct: a canal or channel that carries water to a town or city

archaeologist: a scientist who studies the past through the relics and ruins left behind by people in the past

Aztecs: a Native American people of central Mexico, who developed a great civilization about 500 years ago

burn at the stake: to tie somebody to a post and burn that person alive in public

Caribbean: the sea lying to the east of Central America. It was named after the Caribs, a Native American people who once lived there.

causeway: an embankment in a lake, or in the sea, that is also used as a path or road

chronicle: a history or record of events

civilization: a society that has made progress in the arts, science, or government

civil servant: somebody who works for the state

Columbus: European explorer born in Genoa, Italy. His Italian name was Christoforo Colombo. The Spanish, for whom he worked, called him Cristóbal Colón.

conquistador: one of the Spanish soldiers who invaded Central and South America. The Spanish word means "conqueror."

coral reef: ridge of hard rock on the sea-bed that is formed from the skeletons of millions of sea creatures

empire: various countries ruled by a single government

fertile soil: soil that is rich in the foods that help plants to grow

flowery war: religious ceremony performed by Aztec warriors

fort: an armed camp with a strong wall around it like a castle

heathen: someone who does not believe in the Christian god

high priest: the most important priest in many religions

Hispaniola: a large Caribbean island that Columbus discovered. Today it is split into two countries, Haiti and the Dominican Republic. Columbus called it La Isla Española, "the island of Spain."

Huitzilopochtli: the Aztec god of war

Incas: the people of Peru whose armies conquered a large part of South America in the 15th and 16th centuries

Indians: name given by Columbus to the Native Americans. He made the mistake of assuming that he was in India.

irrigation: a way of taking water from a river, lake, or well to fields so that crops can grow

maize: a tall plant that produces corn

massacre: slaughter, the killing of many people

litter: a box with a seat inside for an important person. It is carried on two poles on the shoulders of a team of men.

Native Americans: the peoples of North, South, and Central America who were already living on those continents before the arrival of Christopher Columbus in 1492, or people descended from them

New World: name given by Europeans to North, South, and Central America. The Old World includes Europe, Asia, and Africa.

plantation: a very large farm estate that is used to grow crops for selling, such as tobacco and sugar cane

plunder: to steal goods and valuables from a conquered town or area

pyramid: a huge, stone building with four sides. Each side is shaped like a triangle. All four come to a point at the top.

Quetzalcoatl: Aztec god with a white face and a dark beard. The name means "feathered serpent."

quipú: a series of colored cords in which knots were tied by Inca clerks to record payments and messages

ransom: money or valuable goods paid in order to free a prisoner from captivity

reinforcements: new soldiers sent to support troops during a battle

rope bridge: bridge made from plaited and twisted straw, which was used by the Incas to cross steep-sided valleys and gorges in the Andes

siege: to surround a town or city and attempt to starve it into surrender

sling: a thong used for throwing stones at high speed

sweet potato: vegetable with a yellow root that grows well in the hot, wet lands of the Americas

tlachtli: a ball game played by the Aztecs on stone courts

tobacco: a plant first grown in the Americas, used for smoking and chewing. Its leaves contain a drug called nicotine.

tribute: forced gifts of money and goods made by a conquered people to their emperor

Vikings: warlike people from Scandinavia who were noted for their skill and daring as seamen. They were the first Europeans to discover America—about 1,000 years ago.